This Grief Coloring Book Belongs To:

Samuel

FREE
APPRECIATION
GIFT IS ON THE
LAST PAGE OF
YOUR COLORING
BOOK

20 Self-Care Tips

1. Take time for self-reflection and journaling
2. Exercise regularly to release pent-up emotions and improve physical and mental health
3. Eat a well-balanced diet to maintain physical health
4. Get plenty of sleep and rest
5. Seek support from family and friends, or attend a support group
6. Allow yourself to feel and express your emotions, rather than bottling them up
7. Practice mindfulness and relaxation techniques like meditation or deep breathing
8. Try to maintain a routine and schedule, but don't be too hard on yourself
9. Participate in activities that bring you joy, like hobbies or spending time with loved ones
10. Seek counseling or therapy to work through your grief and emotions
11. Avoid substance abuse and excessive alcohol consumption
12. Practice self-compassion and be kind to yourself
13. Limit exposure to negative news and media
14. Seek professional help if needed, such as a grief counselor or therapist
15. Take time for self-care, such as taking a relaxing bath or getting a massage
16. Avoid making big life decisions during the grieving process
17. Try to maintain a healthy work-life balance
18. Reach out to community resources, such as religious organizations or local support groups
19. Surround yourself with positive and supportive people
20. Remember that healing is a journey and be patient with yourself.

A Letter To My Loved One

A Letter To My Loved One

_____

_____

_____

_____

_____

_____

_____

_____

_____

_____

_____

_____

_____

_____

_____

_____

_____

A Letter To My Loved One

_____

_____

_____

_____

_____

_____

_____

_____

_____

_____

_____

_____

_____

_____

A Letter To My Loved One

_____

_____

_____

_____

_____

_____

_____

_____

_____

_____

_____

_____

_____

_____

_____

COLOR TEST PAGE

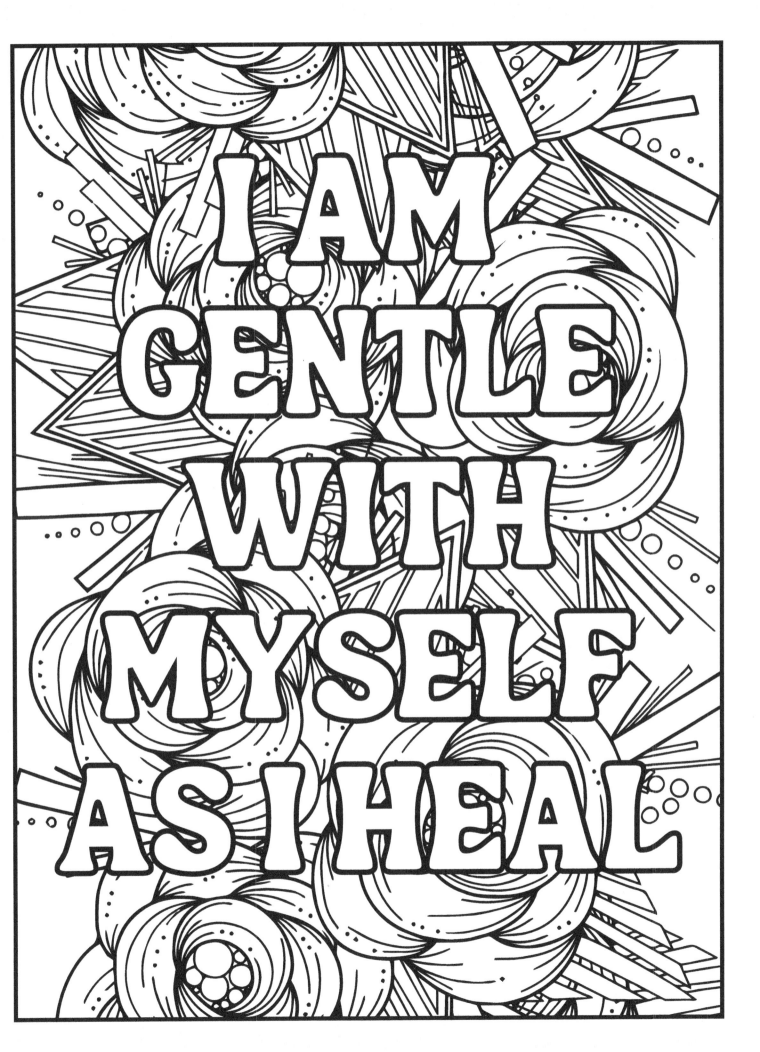

THANK YOU SO MUCH FOR YOUR PURCHASE! HERE IS A THANK YOU GIFT.

SCAN THE QR CODE OR TYPE IN THE URL.

HTTP://BIT.LY/3JRJ4OJ

Made in the USA
Las Vegas, NV
03 May 2023